MORE
SALT
THAN
DIAMOND

MORE
SALT
THAN
DIAMOND

POEMS

ALINE MELLO

Andrews McMeel
PUBLISHING®

For you, immigrant girl.

what did i see to be except myself?
i made it up
        —Lucille Clifton

PROLOGUE

When I was little, I imagined I could control the wind. I would stand in the gathering of trees beyond the parking lot of our apartment building, arms by my side, and listen to a growing rustle, feel for a movement of my arm hair. When I sensed the wind was coming, I'd raise my arms as if I'd called it forth. My hair would rise with the gust, and I'd stay that way—arms raised, hair wild, wind lacing through my fingers until my senses would tell me it was almost over. I would lower my arms according to the speed of the wind. And the moment would be gone. I imagined it just enough that sometimes I believed it. I believed there was something just beyond reach, and that if I discovered it, my whole life would change.

This belief kept me going for a long time. A wooden stick could be a magic wand, a father could return after leaving, a new immigration law could be signed any day now.

When I Say I Want to Go Back

I mean in time.
I want to reach so far back

my arms return to me.
I mean when I pull the thread,

that in the unraveling,
dead grandparents and red dirt and my language

would come back to me.
I mean every time I think of home, I think

of the funerals and pregnancies
and elections and heartbreak

I missed.
I mean the word *home* reminds me of

the pet rabbit my sister swears was blue—
and what if it was?

What I mean to ask is,
how much is time travel anyway?

I'm saying I'd pay
with my English, my Spanish.

I'd trade in my books, my American dogs.
These twenty-three years unlived.

I Will Be an Animal

> "These aren't people. These are animals.
> And we're taking them out
> of the country at a level and at a rate that's never
> happened before."
> —Donald Trump, May 2018

When the president calls you an animal,
you thank him and turn into
a whale, hidden in deep blue.

You move slowly. There's no point in rushing
when you take this much space.
When they let you.

Sometimes you sink into the yawning
to see how far you can swim from the surface,
from the painful gasp of light.

It Is Not Unnatural to Emigrate

The adults are crying
in the airport, so I cry too.

—

There's a movement to life that birds
can't shake. They leave for better
weather, for survival,
but they return.

Ask them to stay for twenty years,
they wouldn't consider it.

—

Twenty-two years ago, I stepped
into an airplane and my tears stopped,
as if I'd been tired of the ground
and flying was the only remedy.

—

A seven-year-old does not know
why she cries, only that others are crying,
and she should join in.

ESL

If you're reading this
in English, it already means

we're far away from each other.
Maybe we're far away together

because English is the only language I write in.
But sometimes my thoughts
pop out in Portuguese,
like from a suitcase
that came with me.
English fills my mouth

with its hard edges, cutting
so it fits better. Can two languages

live inside one person
without bumping into each other?

Does one spread its legs,
limbs stretched like branches,

forcing the other to pull its skin closer to its
bones—
does that one become thin?

The first time I dreamt in English,
I was happy—
a sign I'd been waiting for.

I'm sorry. Eu não sabia.

Sometimes even my tios and primos
speak English in my dreams.

English taking jobs.
English filling the rooms my grandparents
should live in.

Eating Disorder Recovery

I am jealous of teen girls sitting
in the waiting rooms with their moms.

Brand new to their bodies
learning how to live in them.

So nice

to learn love before sadness becomes more
like your scalp than your hair

before shame becomes
stones and sinks to the bottom of your feet

before hate turns its head
toward the mirror.

How do I kill my enemy?
It is me.
It is me.

High School

When the boy asks if Brazil even has universities,
I say yes without thinking,
without telling him I'd never seen one.

He asks of jungles.
"Brazil doesn't have monkeys running in the streets,"
I say, but I've never been to Amazonas, and in Rio
maybe monkeys do dangle from trees nearby,
waiting to yank the pastel from your hands.

I try to keep my country
from being too foreign.

I don't say I think my grandfather still rides his horse
to the store. I want to ask the boy the difference
between monkeys in trees and deer on the roads.
I glare instead.

I must keep my roots intact, so I'll have
something whole to return to.

Mamãe Doesn't Remember the Dictatorship

it ended before I was born,
so I read about it and listen

to the music, remember the words
when I go to the consulate

to vote for anyone but the man
who remembers the dictatorship,

remembers it fondly

To People Who Believe the Earth Is Flat

If the earth has an edge, surely it is lined
with benches, picnic tables—for stopping, waiting, meeting.

I understand.

There must be a place to rest.
Looking for love on a sphere, you'd walk forever.

If there's an edge, it is beauty and horror,
the end, the mouth—where would it lead?

Can a flat Earth hold giants? Oceans?
Or would it sink, heavy with life, soaked through with salt?

If it fell, would it turn like a blade, head toward the sun,
slice through flat moons, flat Mercury?

The Notebook

If you're a bird, I'm not a bird. I'm a planet.
But if you're a planet, I'm a dishrag, a shoe, or pencil.
If you're in love, I am hungry. I'm frustrated in traffic,
asleep.
If you'll confess, then I'll confess: I could never love,
not like love asks.
Love wants too much, and I have these
tiny moles around my eyes I don't want
anyone to see. I want too much
safety, and love doesn't make that promise.
If you confess, I'll confess
it's not worth it.
Love is like a volcano erupting, destroying whole cities,
and me thanking the creeping lava for the views.

Reluctant Love Poem #102

Swimming in space,
do we feel big? Or like stones
moving through black jelly?

I measure the space between
my uncles, my father, and me,
between country and country.

Next (I can't help myself), I'll think
of the space between you and me.

But I don't imagine crossing it,
of how your hand would feel
on my lower back,

if the collar of your shirt smells
like sweat and cologne and detergent.

I won't think of how long your clothes stay warm
without you—did you know we become taller

in space? Gravity isn't there to press us.
And *astronaut* means sailor of stars,
but there is no wind in space.

I imagine a silence so sharp, a sailor
would feel it on her arm hair.

Who would dare travel between star and star,
between confession and confession

and body and body
without wind and sound? Without singing?

In the Reunion of All My Selves

The one still in Brazil does all the cooking,
has yellow turmeric stains under her nails.
The one still in church insists we pray

before we eat, dares someone to say no,
sits beside the one with tattoos
and listens to stories she deems mistakes.

One of us has forgotten
Portuguese but uses Spanish to get by.
One says science and magic are the same,

hands out pamphlets for the new planet
she is building, says everyone would be welcome.
One sends a letter in her stead. She hasn't left home

in decades, couldn't work up the nerve
to make this exception. She sends her regards.
Over a meal of molho de frango spread over white rice,

the women who are me do not ask each other questions.
They are afraid. Instead, they complain about time,
never admitting the longing to switch lives,

and decide to go back to what they know, even if it's all fire.
Even if all they know is burning.
But outside, before goodbyes, the one who's a witch

creates a bonfire, insists they all stand in a circle,
and as the one who's a singer sings
their favorite song, their held hands become

more water than flesh,
bodies more dust than solid,
and in their swaying, the women slip

into oneness,
like a foot slides into an old shoe,
and for a moment, all my selves are whole.

Tired of Speaking English

I go to my mother's kitchen hoping
she needs help peeling garlic.

How rich it is to tire of a language
and have another to run to.

My sister's accent never left her.
She kept a close enough eye
not to lose it.

When I tell Mamãe I get tired
of being lost in crowds of white people,
she says maybe she brought me to the wrong country.

Oh, Georgia

Your summer days are so wet,
I plunge into outside

and I'm swimming.
Picking muscadines,

I wonder who gave me the right
to take from the earth the juicy bulbs.

I swallow your honey and hope
for easier allergies. I slow down

my English when we pull over
during road trips and walk into small

towns, expecting sirens and announcements
in the streets. But I say, *yes, ma'am,* and, *no, sir,*

slowly enough that my tan skin
doesn't cause alarm. Maybe I just stayed out

in the sun too long. Georgia, when I go south,
I need to see your Spanish moss clinging

to the tree branches. Need to taste the saltiness
in the damp air. I want to shake you

like a picnic blanket, free you from your past.
But I cannot.

Will not.
I am here for your wholeness.

Your sneaky laws that make me less safe.
The power you pass down to your white sons.

My Eating Disorder Is a Thin White Woman

Collar bones pushing up like flowers,
skin sinking at the cheeks,

she is pure, hollow
and hungry. But hunger is power.

My eating disorder dreads death.
Not because of death

itself. (She has no time
to ponder the afterlife.)

She fears a fat, relaxed body filling the box,
stomach not sucked in, double chin, thick thighs

touching. She insists I be thin before I die.
Or demands a closed casket instead.

To My Father, on His Birthday

There is a snowstorm in Manhattan today.
I know because I've seen pictures,
and the first day of spring was yesterday.
(Or is it today? I can never remember,
but I know spring reminds me of you.)
But isn't the Arctic melting?
And won't Miami be underwater soon?
And wasn't the phone call you made ten years ago
from the Miami airport?

What if I called today?
Yes, our dog is old but still alive.

No, I broke up with him soon after you left—
Yes, I think he's fine. I don't think he's married.
No, we don't talk anymore.

I know I'm getting older and maybe you
need to say you want grandchildren.
But let's not waste time on that today, Amilton.

Today, we'll talk about Russia because
you've been reading up so we'd have
something to talk about.

Today, you can explain to me Brazilian political parties
and the upcoming elections.

Today, I can sing you a sad song over the phone,
and you won't understand the words,
but you'll cry anyway, and we'll both
ignore the catch and tremor in your voice.

Brasil

They say, *Deus é brasileiro,*
and how can we prove that he isn't?

Maybe Cristo Redentor steps down from his perch
to have cafézim sometimes, unrecognizable.

If the Lord wants to be invisible, who can stop him?
If the Lord craves coxinha com catupiry

and a Guaraná, who would deny him?
The barzim would give him a deal,

add a caipirinha on the house.
Deus é brasileiro and our Seleção proves it.

His stone son, away from the cross,
wrapping his arms around Rio de Janeiro,

celebrating Carnaval. God, may your embrace
bring us more than World Cup trophies.

Excused Absences

Yeah, I would have marched but
not that Saturday you see
the day before there were
explosions inside me
grape tomatoes squeezed between
dull teeth seeded jelly covered
everything
my head got stuck
to the sopped pillow
I'm still cleaning up the mess.

Must be nice to be a
citizen to wear a
shirt that says
"RELAX, GRINGO . . . I'M LEGAL"
my lips bend faster than my brain—
the joke
the shirt
are not for me.

Must be easy to float
to an international airport
home of the officers who move too slow
to my white stepfather's liking
holding a sign that says
WE ARE ALL AMERICAN
when you wake up on the right side of the border.

I couldn't march.
I have a standing appointment with
Mamãe in her kitchen
relating and translating
news articles
reminding her
that she is not white
that I am not safe.

The Country inside Me

is better than the one I left, the one I'm in.

It has no paperwork. The sky isn't limited
to ceiling—it surrounds
everything with all of itself.

Every tree has mangos, and every mango
is sweet.

There, my shoulders forget themselves,
and I make fists only when I'm clutching
new flowers for my mother.

People there know how to greet me:
in English, no pause before my name.

Mamãe Used to Make Dolls

out of corn—
small hands holding
dry, seedless bodies
dressed in leaves,
golden silk carefully combed atop their heads

The Refugee

What pushes a woman
toward the ocean
to go from standing to floating—

what stops her, mid-wash
sends her from home
from her mother

what leads a woman
to pursue an endless blue blindness
if not violence?

DACA

They'll say it was for us
to give us more time
while they made up their minds
on our price tag.

They'll say we have to be thankful
that in a world where plastic
costs so much, they allowed us a piece.

They'll say the others weren't worthy.
That we shouldn't worry.
They'll get their chance one day.

Responsibilities of the Immigrant

here, we must be thankful
for each day they don't see us,
don't notice we are

here, in the home of the brave,
we hide and keep our heads down,
and there's no complaining—

didn't we choose this?
didn't we leave something
and cross another—

didn't we fight for this?
so we number our blessings, and the first
needs to be the English language.

the second must be opportunity,
vague and sacred,
to see power from this side of land and water.

third is the superior culture,
the politeness, the cordial ways
Americans choose to lie.

My Grandmother

would sprinkle water
on the packed dirt

would brush away the clumps
that rose from the earth

with a broom made of long straw

would sweep away the children's residue
stray rocks and grass dragged in

how she cleaned her floors—

still dirt.

Mamãe Smells Like Garlic

peeled with clean, clear nails
crushed in mortar and pestle.
Her hands stained by turmeric,
yellow sinking into the lines,
flavor that doesn't wash away
with soap and water.

Sweat

My body drips, leaves itself behind—
maybe it knows,
like a body knows of its shadow,

knows of other bodies,
that each abandoned drop
might gather with other left things—

like skin cells and backs of earrings
and hair strands and flecks of hardened nail polish—
to form a settlement, accepting of sweat

and salt and moles and fat,
the things bodies can't help but do,
bodies can't help but be.

Studying for the Citizenship Test with My Mother

Sitting with my mother, labeling branches
judicial, executive

The trees outside sway with the hard wind,
and we have to stay inside today, or the leaves
would fly from the balcony, her notecards, her pencils

She asks me the difference between
a citizen's rights and responsibilities

I translate the oath to Portuguese

You'll leave all allegiances to Brazil,
you'll take arms for the US if you need to.
I stop at *So help me God.*

She asks if it's a prayer
I say yes.

Imagine You're Not Alone

You will need more than one bag of yucca flour.

Count ten eggs.

If your mother cannot join you,
if you have no daughter,
learn how to break the shells with one hand.

You will boil milk and oil.

When you sink your hands into the dough,
think of the hands that were there before yours.

Imagine you're holding them.

Alien

I am trying to understand a whole planet,
to add up clouds,
account for each bird

in every city. I do not mind being alone
with my books—solitude
comes like the sun in the east, the craving

for coffee more familiar than wanting company.
And men? Of course they don't see me—
aliens are not women. We are more and beyond.

When I travel
I do not count in miles,
but in breaths, measuring how many

between where my mother is and where I am,
and where I'm going. The grandmother I never met
comes with me, like alien grandmothers tend to do.

She shows up in the taste of rapadura in coffee,
in old Black ladies who call me "baby girl,"
and in my elderly dog who follows me around when I get sick.

But sometimes
she's just light and breath, and it's easy for an alien
to forget that belonging doesn't have to mean place.

My Room Is America

The painting of flying pigs
is the American Dream. The piles
and piles of books are the purple mountains.
This room is my room. This room
is your room. But it's more mine

than yours. My witch's hat is what I wear
when I make decrees. "This mound of clothes,
ignored and stepped on,
wouldn't have such a hard time of it if
it picked itself up from the floor,"
I say. My lamps applaud and agree.

America is my room. And the flag
has a succulent on it. And we pledge allegiance
to a plant that barely needs water.
It is hard to kill. I go to sleep
in my bed, a crucial
part of America, and have no nightmares.
In my room that is America, nothing haunts me.

Mamãe Goes to the Immigration Lawyer

She knows the laws but is not a believer.
She's used to religion,
She will pray—
She will pray—
She will pay for good news.

How Do I Say Goodbye a Second Time?

The wheels, reluctant,
the plane
doing laps around the track
like a bus

the boy behind me
Mickey hat on
whines,
Quando que vai começar voar?

I ask for more time
making my body heavier
pressing down on the seat.

So I can feel it—
the last moments on the ground of my
country

this time
and know what it feels like to leave.

Salt Water

You will be at the beach,
laboring your heels into the sand.

Your mother will talk about her father,
how he'd cook her carne de sol when she'd visit.

You will ask, "Was it worth it? Immigrating?"

She will say things aren't as good back home.
We recreate our homeland in our minds.

She'll tell you it wasn't a mistake.

Squinting in the sunlight, you will wonder
what part ocean, what part sweat, and
what part tears is the salt on your tongue.

I Didn't Know I Didn't Know

My father's love wasn't love but habit,
liturgical movements, a memorized song,
a ritual of words hummed in his mind like music,
beads of sweat building on his forehead.

Liturgical movements, a memorized song.
Love that wasn't love but dance,
beads of sweat building on his forehead,
he moved, holding fragile things in balance.

Not love but dance,
choreography his body knew by rote,
holding fragile things in balance,
every spill folded into rhythm.

The choreography his body knew by rote
looked like love, but I just didn't know,
watching spills fold into rhythm,
that a father's lack stains like oil.

Could have been love, but I didn't know
that every fabric is marked
by a father's lack, stains like oil,
dark droplets hidden in the folds.

Pillar of Salt

It's not her fault she looked back,
the fire made her back sweat, the screams.
Who wouldn't?

Forced to leave what she made into home,
the unfinished quilt, the heirlooms
for her daughters.

When an immigrant leaves
she must look back to make sure

leaving is worth it.

The sin of the immigrant is leaving
and being thankful she left.

Anchor Babies

We can't have it both ways,
can't erase borderlines like kicking
at shoe streaks and say, *here*
is where we belong.
If there are no borders, what is here?
Yes, the water agrees.

It moves from valleys to rain
to oceans, waving, laughing
at barriers. What is a shoreline
but a detour sign? I will not pretend

to know where any of us belongs.
But water breaks without knowing
about countries. And on paper
that's all that matters. Do I blame
pregnant mothers for rushing
toward edges, changing what they can?

If Only Caetano Veloso Knew
He Was Singing to Me

with his soft tenor voice
calling me linda,

asking me to look at time
passing outside the window.

When he says I've left him
alone for so long that he might

be tempted to look elsewhere for love,
I understand.

Decades ago, I left.
Only been back once.

Didn't even tell him.
I wanted to see him

when he came to Miami
but I had a work thing.

When he cries, "Você não me ensinou
a te esquecer," the truth is I can't teach

something I've never learned.
And in my breakup letter, I'll confess

I'm afraid of love, of men,
of what we would do with all the singing.

What Was the Passion Fruit Named
before the Europeans Renamed It?

Before the Christians saw their lord
in its flower, a clock in its tendrils?
How did the natives see the plant's wild curls,
hard petals, little hammers stretching?

How does a child learn to pluck the flower
to separate its body from its body
sitting cross-legged in the dirt
waiting for her mother to call her in?

When does a child, waiting for her father,
come to know that when she pulls
the blossom's ten petals,
her counting will start with "he loves me,"
and always end with "loves me not"?

Reluctant Love Poem #103

You should know
I'm not willing to choose love
enough to trade more than looks,

to meet you
outside the stories I tell of us
to myself. But I'm the reasonable one.

To fall, to be smitten—there's a reason
they choose violent words, you know.
Outside, there are places

to visit and maybe we'd both
stare at the same painting in a museum
for too long—have you thought

of the violence of love? And how we're told
to not wear any armor? Maybe I'm not
foolish enough to show up for the breaking.

Watching My Mother Age

Who did my mother's mothers love?
Who got under their skin, made
their home in there?

Skin darker than mine, uneven,
stained by the sun, by the children,
the crops.

A tree's rings reveal its history.
A mother's folds reveal—what?

How tired she is.
How close to death.

I pinch my mother's skin,
soft on her hand,
and I press it down again, back into place.

Perhaps, like paper, her skin holds memory.
Perhaps it will hold together.
I'm selfish. I want to die first.

I Still Don't Know How to Break a Chicken

How many pieces does one body yield?
If you get the number right, you can have your
own house,
the women say, your own
kitchen, your own man to feed.

I try.
But I break bone and miss the joint,
and the pink, cold flesh is tainted red.

My mother stops me and assigns me
the easiest task: ripping the skin from flesh,
the bumps slippery between my fingers.

I yank and bet she was a perfectly good chicken.
She didn't deserve to be pulled apart, skinned.

Maybe she'd considered running away, just before.
Maybe she'd taken a lover.

But my hands don't stop their violence.
They don't know where my head has gone.

Reluctant Love Poem #113

We could've been like milk and cinnamon.
But we won't call it love.
Calling it love would necessitate more poems,
and I'm tired of grief.

We won't call it love.
Maybe I only ever liked your hands.
I'm tired of grief,
of migraines, of my own body.

I only ever liked hands
that make music, dig up dirt to bury seeds,
my migraines, my whole body.
You had me questioning God.

Let us make music, bury seeds.
Americans believe being grounded is punishment.
You had me. Questioning God,
I crushed garlic and fried it in oil.

Americans believe being grounded is punishment,
and I haven't read enough to argue. Instead,
I crushed garlic and fried it in oil,
poured in the rice and beckoned my grandmother to come.

I haven't read enough, but I still argue
with everyone who asks if I speak Spanish.
Pouring rice always beckons my grandmother.
I'll only speak Spanish with you.

Everyone asks if I speak Spanish.
I can't say I can't.
But I only speak Spanish with you.
We could've been like leite e canela.

Prayer

They said you died so I wouldn't have to.
They said suicide is unforgivable—
there'd be no time, they said,
to ask for forgiveness—tell me

that after the edges of my body
can no longer contain me, there'll be no time
to linger by the oldest trees, to find
my grandmother's grave and whisper its location
in my sister's dreams—tell me

you wouldn't stop if I called you, wouldn't
hold my hand if I said, "Forgive my death,
forgive me. We were done at different times."

Prayer or Blasphemy

Our Mother in Heaven,
may your name be untainted
by people who claim violence.

Mother in Heaven—
calling you *father* dooms you to failure.

May your queendom come soon.
Maybe calling you *she* will draw me closer—

may you draw us closer.
Give us today the nourishment we need
may it run out tonight—
may we return tomorrow.

May your will be done on earth as in heaven.
Forgive us our sins as we forgive
those who will never ask for forgiveness.

Blasphemy

At the beach, I think of Iemanjá—
if she'd ever come this far north.

Called *demon* early in my indoctrination,
now I ask which woman is not a monster

when scared men tell the stories.
Iemanjá, goddess of the ocean, keeper

of my country, do you ever check
on the diaspora? Do you travel to different

shores, searching for Portuguese?
For that familiar rhythm?

God Is Love

of country of guns
and rules and forgiving
forgetting what made him human.
The feeling of fullness,
the stomach heavy and satisfied.
How do I carry it? God is love,
not man. He doesn't remember
sweat and sleep. Earth was a brief,
dark time he has moved on from.

It Is Not Easy to Stay Inside a Body

before, you were water in a river
you run up against the sides like you used to

but there's no release

sometimes, when your body floats
in the ocean, your heart stops
beating

your skin becomes thin
you are almost there

All the Space I Take

in the airplane, wishing I could suck
my hips in. Wishing for a longer seatbelt,
bigger bladder or bigger bathrooms.

In my family, my depression pushing
me down, spreading me out until
I'm under everybody's feet.

I take up space I shouldn't
by standing here, a sliver against
the wall, a stain. Could've been
space for an American citizen.
Could've been thinner. Less.

When I can't back up into myself
anymore, I advance toward me,
hands out, to push at all sides.

And if I happen to trip, to
offer a hug instead, I make
sure to squeeze past comfort.
Maybe this is how I'll fit.

Pão de Queijo

Scoop the dough with a spoon. It will come
half-shaped, ready to be smoothed by your hands,

transformed in the heat.
Your grandmother baked it in her iron oven,

her mother on stones.
But you, with your grated Mexican cheese,

imported polvilho, glass pans,
keep the temperature at 350

and wait for the timer to go off.
You, with your English thoughts

and American ways, can't remember
what your body should know.

How to dig into rich earth for mandioca.
How to wait for milk to become cheese.

But you try.
And at least you don't buy them frozen.

Self-Portrait

I am more water than oil, more salt
than diamond, than quartz. When I am alone,
I am a moon longing for collision.

Alone, I cast my mind like a net,
pull in glitter and darkness. I want
to say I am a whole country. I want
to be a forest of trees. A bird flying

from ground to air to nest—
I too want to feed babies, hide them under my wings.
But I am more wind than bird.

When I am tired of moving, I become a giant,
a whale, and I count my progress in moans,
the space between
my eyes and my tail.

A Giant Sleeps Alone

It's hard
enough finding space for one. A giant

often underestimates her largeness, hoping
she's imagining it, wanting to forget.

But a giant still does the best
she can, and is always on time

for work, though she walks
everywhere, counts her steps, wears a Fitbit

around her pinky toe. Instead of wondering
if one day she'll shop the stores in the mall,

the giant listens to audiobooks on self-help
and gut health. The letters in magazines

are too small, but she likes the pictures
and imagines she was the size of models.

I Am Trying to Keep My Body

alive with insulin and antidepressants,
and therapy and process groups.
I am drowning in thread
and yarn and paint.
Today, staying alive

requires a sewing machine
and maroon knit fabric
and ibuprofen for my back
and YouTube videos.
I text my mother to tell her

I'm still doing my best
to stay awake, still
spending all my money.
She calls to ask what I've eaten today.
I tell her everything from the fridge,

send her pictures of my hands stained red
from beets and black cherries. I want
to hear her say
I am beautiful now.
Want to stand small beside her

as she pinches my side.
To hear her say, *that's enough*
again. But I am
ten years and one hundred pounds
beyond my mother's taste.

One Day When

the birds lift
off their restraints, and keep flying,
maybe we will notice.

Oh, to jump off
and let go, like shedding old shoes
with each step past the threshold.

They say we can keep from crying
by pressing on a spot on our hands,
by breathing in four, holding seven, releasing eight.
But for what?

The more I shed, the lighter
I become.
I become
less afraid of the dark.

Mamãe Is More Like Salt Crystals than Diamonds

yet she begs me to be unbreakable
so that she gets to stay whole

Mother Citizen

She has flowers on her dress
and a blue blazer.
Her hand is cold

but she raises it like a flag.
Makes the necessary promises.

I don't know when I should stop
taking pictures—how many shots
of your mother leaving
does a daughter need?

Her hand lowers and she
smiles at what she's begun.

But Be Transformed

A tadpole becomes a frog. A caterpillar: butterfly,
moth. The body becomes more when we let it.
When we're not afraid. But does the butterfly

dream of bark against her torso, does she miss
the security of land? In the dark, when the flies
are asleep and the night has stopped buzzing,

does the frog dive under the lily pads
to swim without legs?

I paint my nails black and wish for days
when dark nails meant demons.

I sip dark liquor and wonder what I'm opening
my body to. God, so preoccupied
with my nails and skirt length, distracted from

my prayers, eyebrows raised at my piercings—
what should I become for you?

Learning to Mother Myself

I tighten my hair tie,
blow on my forehead to cool
myself down. I wipe the smudges
off my glasses with the soft
cloth I keep in plastic in my purse.

I make sure I have
fresh rice and beans to eat, fry
an egg to add some protein, make
a list and include okra
and milk and even Oreos and even
Hot Pockets. I threaten

to call my father after what he
said to me, give him a piece
of my mind, make him cry too.
I rush home after a painful
day and make sweet, milky
porridge, needle and thread and
cloth ready for crafts and
off-season Christmas music.

Learning to mother myself, I walk
with cleaning supplies, opening
doors, letting myself
into new spaces. I won't turn
on the light, but I'll flip the blinds.
While my mother cleans, the sun
can warm me up.

Tear Gas at the Border

Are we guilty
of trying to make maps work

in our favor?
Trying to cover distances

with only our feet?
This urge to seek promised land

will lead us only to walls
and wild animals

and weapons—will we climb?
Fight? Kill? For what?

Beyond the wall,
there are only more walls,

the first just a warning,
an apology, and a goodbye.

A Really Bad Day

A reflection on the Atlanta shooting, March 16, 2021

My last one came with a migraine,
my head too fragile to move.

I had to fling my body from my bed.
I did not buy a gun.

My temptation is a thirty-year-old man
with good hands and long, black hair.

It's a flight, bought on my phone,
calling me away from this country.

I wouldn't be allowed back in.
It's the ocean, promising me

a beautiful death whenever I'm ready,
just a long walk in.

I did not shoot the man, my phone, the ocean.

When Looking for Home

I look for soft
earth to dig into. A couch
to sink into with books
and saltine crackers

and no choosing a language.
Just me without words. My sounds
and silence enough to earn a name.

A bedroom.
A playground.

I want small signs of belonging.
A child's arms reaching up.

A thoughtless *we*
that comes with habitual love.

Sister

When we speak Portuguese, our voices
are the same, echoes of our mother's.

In a room filled with people who say
we look more like cousins, you are

a planet. You have your own pull, and I
become a moon. Sister, what is this

sticky comfort that comes with knowing you
know me? My father left me, and so did
yours.

I was made to leave my country behind,
and you came too. We wore handmade

clothing to the airport. Linen. With hats,
like we were from another time. I know you

can sing and choose not to. I know you
ignore your anxiety until it takes over

your body. There is so much unsaid.
But we don't want to say it.

And we can blame our father for choosing
between us. In the end, we will sit in a station,

watch the trains go by. And there will be you.
And there will be me.

If I Ever Get My Citizenship Papers

How is it for a dolphin to be set free,
that first dive into wild water,
never finding the bottom,

no more faces or hands against glass—
Would she miss the music, the dancing?
Flip for fish, wait for reward from above?
Would she sink too far from breath?

Allegiance

I pledge allegiance to the air and
wind even in spring, when it stresses

my allergies, it is still unassuming,
vital, doing its best.

To the land before country, when borders
were rivers and mountains.

To my mother, keeper of my language,
my name. She is rock and foam.

To the ocean, the way it speaks to the moon,
pushes against the earth. Draws it in.

To the birds that find their way over buildings,
know when to leave and when to stay.

Mamãe Is Not White

how do I tell her?
how do I point at her skin—
call it alien
and not my own?

Brasil #2

When I can't scrub a country from my skin,
I sink into wrinkled white flags,
into memories of boiled chickens,
my hands full of wet feathers.
I did not like the smell.

I taste cool water from clay filters,
thick milk, still warm before the sky
gave up its stars. Yes, I remember
how I got the scar above my knee,
the one above my belly button—a country
is like a father on the phone asking
if you've forgotten you have a father.

Our backyard was dirt until my father made it cement
and falling started costing more.
What is the point of forgetting?
Walking into banks to feel the air-conditioning
cool your sweat, just to feel the wall of heat
when you walk out again.

What is my country but property people fought for?
What is my country but a tug-of-war?

I like to think we will lose to the forests.
One day, the trees will say *enough*.
The Amazon River will ignore its banks.
And we will try to burn the trees, to drink the rivers,
but a small group of knowers will kneel
and say, "Esperávamos por isso,"
but in a language that has never belonged to colonizers.

Reluctant Love Poem #109

Before I go
before I pull it all up from the roots,
before I realize the danger of staying here,
being looked at by you—
you should say your piece
while I'm still listening.

When it comes to being afraid,
I will always win.
I've seen you see it.
And I've let you close enough.

So, before it's over,
before I run,
you should try to speak forever.

I will wait until you finish.

My Poems Turn to God

in the end, like they say
we all will,
like the rain,
after free-falling
to earth, will
drag itself up
in mist
eventually.

I'm Tired of Seeing Brown Children Crying on the News

Let their tears turn into a river
only they can play in.

Let their hands reach for hands
reach for hands.

Let them make a circle in the emptied warehouse,
backs turned to everyone else, brown eyes on brown eyes—
let them see something older and stronger than themselves.

Is this a prayer?

If the ancestors can hear me, I ask you for company,
remind me this isn't all there is.

If God can hear me, let it not be the cold white
god of the Christians—the one who glows
while walking down the street,
who can't figure out what to do with his hair.

Let it be the brown one who knows wounds,
who knows crying.

If this god can hear me, let us be
someplace else.

We would be fine someplace among the stars—
just darkness and bright, our skin so hidden and illuminated,
no one would know what to call it—

And So Let Us Imagine a New Country

With fruit trees lining every street
and gardens and cows and chickens on every block.

Neighbors feeding neighbors, and everyone is a neighbor.
With statues of women holding children and men

tending flowers.
Hands filled with seeds and fragile things.

Every light a sun or a moon. Every liquid a river, a lake.
Where we can turn off the moon now and lie together

on the thin, green mattress that is grass, under a comforter—
there's no better word for comforter.

Let us imagine a place that stretches beyond
lines drawn on maps by men long dead.

A country is but a people
under a piece of cloth with lines and colors.

A country is land that has soaked up blood
after blood.

A country is nothing but space limited and cut.
Let us not be reduced to countries.

We will meet where everyone drinks lakes of juice,
sit by blossoms, watch the

sun sink low. The moon returns
and reminds us there is still time.
There is still time.

I Belong to Myself

I must become my own
home to return to.

When asked, "Where are you?"
Say, "I am here."

And when I feel the earth
could let go at any point,

relax its hold on me, I reach
across my chest, my hand

squeezing my own shoulder,
and say, "I know, I know."

And when asked, "What are you?"
Answer, "Here—I am here."

NOTES

Mamãe Doesn't Remember the Dictatorship
In 1964, Brazilian military forces were backed by the CIA
to overthrow the left-wing then-president, João Goulart.
The dictatorship that was subsequently established led
to two decades of violence, murder, and torture. The
current president of Brazil, Jair Bolsonaro, has repeatedly
lamented the fall of the Brazilian dictatorship.

Pillar of Salt
Genesis 19:15-26

If Only Caetano Veloso Knew He Was Singing to Me
In this poem, I allude to a few of Caetano Veloso's songs:
"Você é linda," "Carolina," "Sozinho," and "Você não
me ensinou a te esquecer."

But Be Transformed
Romans 12:2

A Really Bad Day
On March 16, 2021, after targeting Asian workplaces
and killing eight people—six of them Asian women—
the murderer was arrested. Afterward, during a news
conference, the speaker for the Cherokee County Sheriff's
Office said, "Yesterday was a really bad day for him and
this is what he did."

ACKNOWLEDGMENTS

There are so many people who have helped this book come to be. And there are those who have helped me become a writer, believe I'm a writer, and stay a writer. I owe my beginnings to the founders and funders of Undocupoets, who questioned the status quo and chose to challenge it. Marcelo Hernandez Castillo, Christopher Soto, Javier Zamora—I am so grateful for your courage. Janine Joseph, Analicia Sotelo, Esther Lin—thank you for sharing your writer wisdom with me and for answering me the times I reached out frantically. Bryan Borland from Sibling Rivalry Press—I still have the note you sent. Cameron Lawrence—much more than a former boss, you became a friend and mentor who was patient yet diligent in convincing me I could write. Thank you to those friends who engaged in conversations with me that led to poetry. I am so fortunate to have friends who ask questions. Amy Hayes, Kayla Yiu, Stefani McDade, Tim Rhodes, Beth Rhodes, Jamie Hughes—thank you for the conversations that led to poems and for being listeners to them when they were still drafts. Then there are those friends who encourage you to dream as high as you can: Diana Chávez, Frances Crusoe, Sunita Theiss, Taina Brown, Quiana Culbreath, Melo Yap— thank you for your steady belief in me. And, yes, to my therapists who work in giving me 150 years' worth of validation, which I so desperately need: Thank you! And thank you to Prozac, of course.

In 2020, a strange and difficult year, I met Paola
Capó-García through the Latinx in Publishing Writers
Mentorship Program. Paola was instrumental in this
book coming together. She is my first Latina poetry
mentor and was the first to call my clumps of poems
a manuscript. I appreciate your guidance and your
Virgo energy. Larissa Melo Pienkowski, my agent, was
another bright light in 2020. Thank you for finding
me and for believing in my work. Thank you to Neil
Aitken for your feedback and for helping me get the
order of the poems right. A thank-you to my editor
Patty Rice and the Andrews McMeel team for getting
behind this group of poems.

Before these poems became this book, several of them
(or versions of them) were published in different
literary journals, anthologies, and books. I would
like to thank the editors from the following journals
and anthologies for giving these baby poems homes:
Atlanta Review, the *Chattahoochee Review, Fare
Forward, From Everywhere a Little: A Migration
Anthology,* the *Georgia Review, Ghost City Review,
Grist, Indiana Review, Latina Outsiders Remaking
Latina Identity, The BreakBeat Poets Vol. 4:
LatiNEXT,* the *New Republic, No Tender Fences: An
Anthology of Immigrant & First-Generation American
Poetry, Palabritas, Quarterly West,* the *Rumpus,
Scalawag, storySouth,* and *Wildness.*

I want to thank my family for never doubting I could
write a book. I claimed this goal as a child, and my
sister and mother believed me then and since. Mamãe,

thank you for coming back to love, even after so much
has tried to pull you away from it. I feel your love for
me every time you say, "Faça o que te faz feliz," every
time you call me "minha flor," every time you help me
clean out the clutter in my room and bathroom. Mara,
I love you like the ocean loves the moon—it's moved
by it; it would be a boring, large, salty puddle without
it. Thank you for being the best possible big sister to
me. Our life brought us close, made us best friends,
made us want to be neighbors and be together always.
I don't regret that. I don't understand anyone who has
you in their life who doesn't want forever with you.
Mark, I wish you'd met my mother sooner. I wish your
encouragement, love, presence, emotional intelligence
had been there in my upbringing. And I'm so thankful
you are here these later years. You're the father I never
had and one everyone deserves.

I'm thankful for my uncles, aunts, cousins, and
grandparents. Some of you, I've never met. Most of
you, I have not really known. But I'm grateful that my
cousin's baby looks like me, that my aunts' posture
is identical to my mom's, that I can imagine so is my
grandmother's. There is a string connecting us to each
other and to those who came before us, and I don't
take that for granted. I'm sorry I rarely call. Perdão. Eu
sei que eu sumo.

INDEX

ABOUT THE AUTHOR

Aline Mello was born in Brazil and emigrated with her family as a child in 1997. Her work often centers on themes of identity, religion, the body, family, and the experience of the self living in diaspora. Her immigrant and undocumented identity have influenced her writing and her art. She is an Undocupoet fellow and a graduate fellow at Ohio State University, and her work can be found in journals such as *Georgia Review, Quarterly West, Indiana Review,* and the *Rumpus.* Visit her on social media at @thealinemello and at www.thealinemello.com.

Imagery by Stephanie Eley

Andrews McMeel Publishing
a division of Andrews McMeel Universal
1130 Walnut Street, Kansas City, Missouri 64106

www.andrewsmcmeel.com

22 23 24 25 26 VEP 10 9 8 7 6 5 4 3 2 1

ISBN: 978-1-5248-7102-4

Library of Congress Control Number: 2021948780

Editor: Patty Rice
Art Director: Tiffany Meairs
Production Editor: Elizabeth A. Garcia
Production Manager: Carol Coe

ATTENTION: SCHOOLS AND BUSINESSES
Andrews McMeel books are available at quantity discounts
with bulk purchase for educational, business, or sales
promotional use. For information, please e-mail the
Andrews McMeel Publishing Special Sales Department:
specialsales@amuniversal.com.